Amazing Avocado: Insanely Breakfast and Dessert Reci_ and Easy Weight Loss

M000103846

by **Alissa Noel Grey**
Text copyright(c)2014 Alissa Noel Grey

All rights reserved. No part of this publication may be reproduced, distributed, or transmitted in any form or by any means, including photocopying, recording, or other electronic or mechanical methods, without the prior written permission of the publisher, except in the case of brief quotations embodied in critical reviews and certain other noncommercial uses permitted by copyright law

Although every precaution has been taken to verify the accuracy of the information contained herein, the author and publisher assume no responsibility for any errors or omissions. No liability is assumed for damages that may result from the use of information contained within.

Table Of Contents

Absolutely Avocados   5
Chicken, Lettuce and Avocado Salad   6
Mashed Avocado and Chicken Salad   7
Beef, Spinach and Avocado Salad   8
Steak Salad with Arugula and Avocado   9
Mediterranean Beef and Avocado Salad   10
Salmon, Avocado and Asparagus Salad   11
Avocado, Asparagus and Cherry Tomato Salad   12
Avocado and Corn Salad   13
Avocado, Black Bean and Red Pepper Salad   14
Avocado and Roasted Balsamic Mushroom Salad   15
Cucumber, Avocado and Sprout Salad   16
Carrot, Avocado and Sprout Salad   17
Arugula and Avocado Salad   18
Arugula and Pomegranate Salad   19
Avocado and Green Bean Salad   20
Beet and Avocado Salad   21
Mediterranean Avocado Salad   22
Avocado and Cucumber Salad   23
Warm Tomato and Avocado Salad   24
Quinoa and Avocado Salad   25
Quinoa, Tomato and Avocado Salad   26
Chickpea and Avocado Salad   27
Avocado Hummus   28
Zucchini and Avocado Hummus   29
Hot Avocado Dip   30
Spicy Avocado Dip   31
Avocado and Feta Dip   32
Avocado and Feta Toast with Poached Eggs   33
Avocado and Olive Paste on Toasted Rye Bread   34
Avocado, Lettuce and Tomato Sandwiches   35
Avocado and Chickpea Sandwiches   36
Avocado, Roast Beef and Lettuce Sandwiches   37
Avocado Gazpacho   38
Avocado and Cucumber Soup   39

Warm Chicken and Avocado Soup   40
Avocado and Arugula Pasta   41
Creamy Avocado and Chicken Spaghetti   42
Avocado, Roasted Mushroom and Ham Spaghetti   43
Avocado and Chicken Risotto   44
Cornmeal Avocado Muffin Recipe   46
Avocado and Banana Muffins   47
Avocado and Pumpkin Muffins   48
Green Apple and Avocado Smoothie   49
Carrot, Mango and Avocado Smoothie   50
Strawberry, Coconut and Avocado Smoothie   51
Delicious Avocado and Plum Smoothie   52
Pumpkin and Avocado Smoothie   53
Pineapple and Avocado Smoothie   54
Kiwi, Grapes and Avocado Smoothie   55
Avocado and Nectarine Smoothie   56
FREE BONUS RECIPES: 20 Superfood Paleo and Vegan
Smoothies for Vibrant Health and Easy Weight Loss   57
Kale and Kiwi Smoothie   58
Delicious Broccoli Smoothie   59
Papaya Smoothie   60
Beet and Papaya Smoothie   61
Lean Green Smoothie   62
Easy Antioxidant Smoothie   63
Healthy Purple Smoothie   64
Mom's Favorite Kale Smoothie   65
Creamy Green Smoothie   66
Strawberry and Arugula Smoothie   67
Emma's Amazing Smoothie   68
Good-To-Go Morning Smoothie   69
Endless Energy Smoothie   70
High-fibre Fruit Smoothie   71
Nutritious Green Smoothie   72
Apricot, Strawberry and Banana Smoothie   73
Spinach and Green Apple Smoothie   74
Superfood Blueberry Smoothie   75

Zucchini and Blueberry Smoothie   76
Tropical Spinach Smoothie   77

Absolutely Avocados

I'll eat an avocado at any time of the day. In fact lately I have become somewhat obsessed with avocados. And that is not because they are incredibly healthy and loaded with important nutrients and are practically one of the healthiest food on the planet.

No, my interest in avocados was aroused when I discovered that they can actually taste amazing when combined with the right foods and spices. The other thing I discovered about avocados, and that is probably what turned me into an enthusiastic fan, is that when I eat avocado for breakfast, lunch or dinner I feel so full and satisfied that I am able to regulate my somewhat crazy appetite.

So, because this is a cookbook, I am not going to repeat the many health benefits of avocados, that are well known and supported by science. Instead I am offering you my favorite recipes featuring that amazing fruit– simple and easy salads, soups, main dishes, smoothies and sandwiches, that I prepare every day and are loved by everyone in my big family.

Chicken, Lettuce and Avocado Salad

Serves: 4-5

Prep time: 5 min

Ingredients:

2 grilled chicken breasts, diced

1 avocado, peeled and diced

5-6 green lettuce leaves, cut in stripes

3-4 green onions, finely chopped

5-6 radishes, sliced

7-8 grape tomatoes

2 tbsp lemon juice

3 tbsp extra virgin olive oil

1 tsp dried mint

salt and black pepper, to taste

Directions:

In a deep salad bowl, combine avocado, lettuce, chicken, onions, radishes and grape tomatoes.

Season with mint, salt and pepper to taste. Sprinkle with lemon juice and olive oil. Toss lightly and serve.

Mashed Avocado and Chicken Salad

Serves: 4-5

Prep time: 5 min

Ingredients:

2 cooked chicken breasts, diced

1 small red onion, finely chopped

2 ripe avocados, mashed with a fork

3 tbsp lemon juice

1 tbsp extra virgin olive oil

1 tbsp fresh tarragon leaves, finely cut

salt and pepper, to taste

Directions:

Place the chicken in a medium sized salad bowl. In a plate, mash the avocados using either a fork or a potato masher and add them to the chicken. Add in the onion, tarragon, lemon juice and olive oil. Season with salt and black pepper, to taste. Stir to combine and serve.

Beef, Spinach and Avocado Salad

Serves 4-5

Prep time: 5 min

Ingredients:

8 oz quality roast beef, thinly sliced

1 avocado, peeled and sliced

1 red onion, sliced and separated into rings

2 tomatoes, thinly sliced

3 cups baby spinach leaves

2 tbsp extra virgin olive oil

salt, to taste

for the dressing:

2 tbsp lemon juice

1 tbsp extra virgin olive oil

1 tbsp mustard

Directions:

Combine dressing ingredients in a deep bowl and whisk until smooth.

Heat olive oil in a large skillet and gently sauté beef and onions. Cook until beef is heated through.

Toss together beef, spinach, tomatoes and avocado in a large salad bowl. Season with salt, drizzle with dressing and serve.

Steak Salad with Arugula and Avocado

Serves 4

Prep time: 7-8 min

Ingredients:

1 lb boneless beef sirloin steak, 1 inch thick

1 avocado, peeled and sliced

3 cups arugula leaves

1 red onion, sliced and separated into rings

1/2 cup feta cheese, crumbled

salt and black pepper, to taste

2 tbsp extra virgin olive oil

for the dressing:

2 garlic cloves, crushed

2 tbsp extra virgin olive oil

1 tbsp balsamic vinegar

1/2 tsp dried basil

salt and black pepper, to taste

Directions:

Prepare the dressing by whisking all ingredients in a bowl.

In a heavy skillet, heat olive oil. Season steak with salt and black pepper and cook for 3-4 minutes, each side, on medium heat. Set aside on a cutting board and leave to cool. Slice against the grain.

Toss the steak with arugula, onion, avocado and feta. Season with salt and pepper, drizzle with dressing and serve.

Mediterranean Beef and Avocado Salad

Serves 4

Prep time: 5 min

Ingredients:

8 oz quality roast beef, thinly sliced

1 avocado, peeled and sliced

2 tomatoes, sliced

1 cucumber, thinly sliced

1 yellow pepper, sliced

3-4 green olives, finely cut

1 cup black olives, pitted and halved

2-3 fresh basil leaves, torn

2-3 fresh oregano leaves

1 tbsp balsamic vinegar

4 tbsp extra virgin olive oil

salt and black pepper, to taste

Directions:

Combine roast beef, avocado and all vegetables in a large salad bowl. Add in basil and oregano leaves.

Season with salt and pepper, drizzle with balsamic vinegar and olive oil, toss to combine, and serve.

Salmon, Avocado and Asparagus Salad

Serves: 4

Prep time: 5 min

Ingredients:

1 cucumber, peeled and chopped

1 avocado, peeled and cubed

1 bunch asparagus, trimmed, cut into 2 inch lengths

1 can salmon, drained and broken into large chunks

1 cup corn kernels, cooked

4 tbsp lemon juice

2 tbsp extra virgin olive oil

1 tbsp dill, very finely chopped

Directions:

Cook asparagus in boiling salted water for one to two minutes or until bright green and tender. Drain, rinse and pat dry. Place asparagus, cucumber, avocado, corn and salmon into a deep salad bowl. Toss to combine.

In a small bowl, whisk together lemon juice, olive oil and dill. Stir in salt and black pepper to taste. Pour over the salad, toss to combine, and serve

Avocado, Asparagus and Cherry Tomato Salad

Serves: 4-5

Prep time: 5 min

Ingredients:

2 avocados, sliced

1 cup baby spinach leaves

1 cup cherry tomatoes, halved

1 bunch asparagus, trimmed and halved

1/3 cup walnuts, halved and toasted

4 tbsp lemon juice

2 tbsp extra virgin olive oil

2-3 green onions, very finely cut

1 tsp dried basil

Directions:

Prepare the dressing by whisking lemon juice, olive oil, green onions and basil in a bowl. Season with salt and black pepper to taste.

Combine baby spinach, tomato, asparagus and walnuts in a bowl. Add avocado and dressing; toss to combine and serve.

Avocado and Corn Salad

Serves: 4

Prep time: 5 min

Ingredients:

2 avocados, peeled and finely chopped

1 can corn kernels, drained

4-5 green onions, finely chopped

3 tbsp chopped fresh parsley

3 tbsp lemon juice

½ tsp cumin

Directions:

Combine avocados, corn, onions, parsley, cumin and lemon juice in a salad bowl and serve immediately.

Avocado, Black Bean and Red Pepper Salad

Serves: 4-5

Prep time: 6-7 min

Ingredients:

2 avocados, peeled and diced

1 can black beans, drained

2 red bell pepper, diced

1-2 green onions, finely chopped

1 garlic clove, minced

3 tbsp chopped fresh coriander

3 tbsp lemon juice

2 tbsp extra virgin olive oil

½ tsp cumin

Directions:

Place avocados, beans, bell peppers, green onions, garlic, coriander and cumin in a salad bowl.

Sprinkle with lemon juice and olive oil, toss to combine and serve immediately.

Avocado and Roasted Balsamic Mushroom Salad

Serves: 4

Prep time: 6-7 min

Ingredients:

10-15 mushrooms, halved

2 tbsp balsamic vinegar

3 tbsp extra virgin olive oil

1 avocado, peeled and sliced

1/2 cup parsley leaves, finely cut

salt and black pepper, to taste

Directions:

Line a baking tray with baking paper and place the mushrooms on it. Drizzle with olive oil and balsamic vinegar. Season with salt and black pepper to taste. Roast in a preheated to 375 F oven for 15 minutes, or until golden and tender.

Combine avocado and mushrooms in a salad bowl. Stir in parsley. Drizzle some more balsamic vinegar and olive oil if desired.

Cucumber, Avocado and Sprout Salad

Serves: 3-4

Prep time: 5 min

Ingredients:

1 avocado, peeled and diced

1 medium cucumber, peeled and diced

1 cup broccoli or sunflower sprouts

5-6 radishes, sliced

1 tbsp roasted pumpkin seeds

for the dressing:

2 tbsp lemon juice

2 tbsp extra virgin olive oil

1 tbsp Dijon mustard

Directions:

Place all ingredients in a large salad bowl and toss until combined.

In a medium bowl, whisk dressing ingredients until smooth. Pour over salad, toss thoroughly and serve.

Carrot, Avocado and Sprout Salad

Serves: 4

Prep time: 5 min

Ingredients:

1 avocado, peeled and diced

1 large carrot, grated

2 cups broccoli or sunflower sprouts

1 garlic clove, minced

for the dressing:

3 tbsp lemon juice

2 tbsp extra virgin olive oil

1/2 tsp salt

Directions:

Place all ingredients in a salad bowl and toss until combined.

In a medium bowl, whisk dressing ingredients until smooth. Pour over salad, toss thoroughly and serve.

Arugula and Avocado Salad

Serves: 4

Prep time: 5 min

Ingredients:

1 bunch arugula leaves

2 avocados, peeled and sliced

2 tomatoes, sliced

1 small red onion, sliced

1 tbsp lemon juice

2 tbsp extra virgin olive oil

salt, to taste

Directions:

Place arugula, avocados, tomatoes and onion in a salad bowl and gently toss to combine. Sprinkle with salt, lemon juice and olive oil, stir, and serve.

Arugula and Pomegranate Salad

Serves: 4-5

Prep time: 5 min

Ingredients:

1 bunch baby arugula leaves

1 small head radicchio, chopped

1 avocado, peeled and cubed

1/2 cup pomegranate seeds, from 1 medium pomegranate

1/3 cup roasted hazelnuts

for the dressing:

1 tbsp honey

1 tbsp balsamic vinegar

2 tbsp extra virgin olive oil

1/2 tsp salt

Directions:

Place baby arugula, radicchio, avocado, hazelnuts and pomegranate seeds in a large salad bowl and gently toss to combine.

Whisk dressing ingredients until smooth, pour over the salad and serve immediately.

Avocado and Green Bean Salad

Serves: 4

Prep time: 10 min

Ingredients:

1 lb trimmed green beans, cut into 2-3 inch long pieces

1 small red onion, finely cut

1 cup cherry tomatoes, halved

1 avocado, peeled and diced

3-4 garlic cloves, chopped

1 tbsp chia seeds

4 tbsp extra virgin olive oil

3/4 cup freshly grated Parmesan cheese

salt and pepper, to taste

1 cup fresh dill, finely cut, to serve

Directions:

Steam or boil the green beans for about 3-4 minutes until crisp-tender. In a colander, wash with cold water to stop cooking, then pat dry and place in a salad bowl.

Add red onion, garlic, cherry tomatoes, and avocado and sprinkle in the chia seeds. Season with lemon juice and balsamic vinegar. Toss to coat, add in the olive oil and Parmesan cheese and toss again. Season to taste with salt and freshly ground black pepper. Refrigerate for an hour and serve sprinkled with fresh dill.

Beet and Avocado Salad

Serves: 4

Prep time: 25 min

Ingredients:

1 avocado, peeled and diced

3 medium beets, steamed and diced

1 red onion, sliced

1/2 cup walnuts, halved

1 tbsp lemon juice

2 tbsp extra virgin olive oil

4-5 mint leaves

½ tsp salt

Directions:

Wash the beets, trim the stems, and steam them over boiling water until cooked through.

Peel, dice and place them in a salad bowl. Add in walnuts, onion, lemon juice and olive oil and toss to combine. Gently stir in avocado, chill for 15 minutes and serve sprinkled with fresh mint leaves.

Mediterranean Avocado Salad

Serves: 5-6

Prep time: 10 min

Ingredients:

2 avocados, peeled and diced

½ ciabatta roll, cut into small cubes

2 cups cherry tomatoes, halved

½ red onion, thinly sliced

1 small cucumber, halved, sliced

½ cup green olives, pitted, halved

½ cup black olives, pitted and halved

1 cup feta cheese, crumbled

7-8 fresh basil leaves, torn

½ cup parsley leaves, finely cut

4 tbsp extra virgin olive oil

3 tbsp red wine vinegar

Directions:

Line a baking tray with baking paper and place ciabatta cubes. Drizzle with one tablespoon of olive oil. Season with salt and pepper and gently toss to coat. Cook under the grill for 2-3 minutes or until golden. Set aside to cool.

Place vegetables, feta, basil, olives, and ciabatta cubes in a large salad bowl. Gently toss to combine then sprinkle with vinegar and remaining olive oil. Season with salt and pepper and gently toss again. Sprinkle with parsley and serve.

Avocado and Cucumber Salad

Serves: 4-5

Prep time: 10 min

Ingredients:

2 avocados, peeled, halved and sliced

½ red onion, thinly sliced

1 large cucumber, halved, sliced

½ radicchio, trimmed, finely shredded

7-8 fresh basil leaves, torn

for the dressing:

1 tbsp black olive paste

2 tbsp extra virgin olive oil

1 tbsp balsamic vinegar

1 tbsp lemon juice

salt and pepper, to taste

Directions:

Combine avocado, radicchio and cucumber in a bowl. Place vinegar, oil, lemon juice and black olive paste in a small bowl and whisk until very well combined.

Pour over the salad, season with salt and pepper and toss gently to combine.

Warm Tomato and Avocado Salad

Serves: 4-5

Prep time: 10 min

Ingredients:

4 tomatoes, sliced

1 cup cherry tomatoes, halved

1 avocado, peeled and sliced

½ small red onion, very finely cut

2 garlic cloves, crushed

1 tbsp dried mint

2 tbsp extra virgin olive oil

1 tbsp balsamic vinegar

Directions:

Gently heat oil in a non-stick frying pan over low heat. Cook garlic and tomatoes, stirring occasionally, for 4-5 minutes or until tomatoes are warm but firm. Remove from heat and place in a plate.

Add in avocado, red onion, vinegar and dried mint. Season with salt and pepper, to taste, and serve.

Quinoa and Avocado Salad

Serves: 4-5

Prep time: 15 min

Ingredients:

1 cup quinoa

2 cups water

1 large avocado, peeled and sliced

¼ radicchio, finely sliced

1 small pink grapefruit, peeled and finely cut

handful of arugula leaves

1 cup baby spinach leaves

2 tbsp extra virgin olive oil

2 tbsp lemon juice

salt and black pepper, to taste

Directions:

Wash quinoa in a fine sieve under running water for 2-3 minutes, or until water runs clear. Set aside to drain, then boil in two cups of water for 15 minutes.

Fluff with a fork and set aside to cool. Stir avocado, radicchio, arugula and baby spinach into cooled quinoa. Add grapefruit, lemon juice and olive oil, season with salt and black pepper, and stir to combine.

Quinoa, Tomato and Avocado Salad

Serves: 4-5

Prep time: 15 min

Ingredients:

1/2 cup quinoa

1 cup water

1 avocado, peeled and diced

2 tomatoes, diced

1 cup baby spinach, washed and dried

2-3 green onions, finely chopped

4 oz crumbled blue cheese

2 tbsp lemon juice

4 tbsp extra virgin olive oil

salt, to taste

Directions:

Wash quinoa in a fine sieve under running water for 2-3 minutes, or until water runs clear. Set aside to drain, boil it in two cups of water for 15 minutes and set aside to cool.

Place the baby spinach leaves in a large bowl and add in tomatoes, green onions and blue cheese. Stir in quinoa. Season to taste with salt, drizzle with lemon juice and olive oil and toss to combine.

Chickpea and Avocado Salad

Serves: 3-4

Prep time: 2-3 min

Ingredients:

1 15 oz can chickpeas, drained, or 1/2 cup dried chickpeas, boiled and drained

1 avocado, peeled and sliced

1 small red onion, chopped

1 cucumber, peeled and diced

2 tomatoes, diced

½ cup fresh coriander, finely chopped

2 tbsp extra virgin olive oil

1 tbsp balsamic vinegar

salt, to taste

Directions:

In a salad bowl, toss together the chickpeas, onion, cucumber, tomatoes and coriander.

Add in the sliced avocado, balsamic vinegar, olive oil and salt. Gently toss to combine and serve.

Avocado Hummus

Serves: 4

Prep time: 2-3 min

Ingredients:

1 15 oz can chickpeas, drained

1 medium avocado, peeled and chopped

2 tbsp tahini

1/4 cup lemon juice

1 garlic clove, crushed

2 tbsp finely cut parsley

1 tbsp extra virgin olive oil

½ tsp paprika

1/2 tsp cumin

salt and pepper, to taste

Directions:

Heat oil in a small frying pan over medium-high heat. Add half the chickpeas and cook, stirring, for 3-4 minutes or until just golden. Remove from heat and set aside to cool.

Blend remaining chickpeas with avocado, tahini, lemon juice, garlic and cumin until smooth.

Season with salt and pepper and spoon the avocado hummus into a serving bowl. Top with chickpeas, sprinkle with paprika and parsley and serve.

Zucchini and Avocado Hummus

Serves: 4

Prep time: 5 min

Ingredients:

1 large zucchini, peeled and diced

1 avocado, peeled and chopped

2 garlic cloves, chopped

2 tbsp tahini

2 tbsp extra virgin olive oil

1/4 cup lemon juice

1 tsp cumin

salt, to taste

Directions:

Combine all ingredients in a blender and pulse until smooth.

Serve with crackers, cut-up fresh vegetables or chips.

Hot Avocado Dip

Serves: 6

Prep time: 5 min

Ingredients:

2 large avocados, peeled and chopped

1/2 small red onion, finely chopped

3 tbsp lemon juice

1/2 tsp cayenne pepper

salt and black pepper, to taste

fresh coriander leaves, chopped, to serve

Directions:

Mash avocados with a fork or potato masher until almost smooth. Add onion, lemon juice and cayenne pepper.

Season with salt and pepper to taste. Stir to combine, top with fresh coriander and serve immediately.

Spicy Avocado Dip

Serves: 6

Prep time: 5 min

Ingredients:

2 large avocados, peeled and chopped

½ cup sour cream

2 garlic cloves, crushed

3 tbsp lemon juice

1 tsp hot sauce

salt and black pepper, to taste

fresh parsley leaves, finely cut, to serve

Directions:

Mash avocados with a fork or potato masher until smooth. Add the sour cream, onion, lemon juice and hot sauce.

Season with salt and pepper to taste. Stir to combine, top with parsley and serve immediately.

Avocado and Feta Dip

Serves: 6

Prep time: 5 min

Ingredients:

2 large avocados, peeled and chopped

1/2 cup feta cheese, crumbled

3-4 green onions, finely chopped

½ red pepper, very finely chopped

1 garlic clove, crushed

1 tbsp lemon juice

salt and black pepper, to taste

3 tbsp dill, very finely cut

Directions:

Mash avocados with a fork or potato masher until smooth. Add the green onions, pepper, garlic, feta, dill and lemon juice.

Season with salt and pepper to taste. Stir to combine and serve immediately.

Avocado and Feta Toast with Poached Eggs

Serves: 4

Prep time: 5 min

Ingredients:

1 avocado, peeled and chopped

½ cup feta cheese, crumbled

2 tbsp chopped fresh mint

1 tsp lime juice

½ tsp cumin

4 thick slices rye bread, lightly toasted

4 poached eggs

Directions:

Mash avocados with a fork until almost smooth. Add the feta, fresh mint, lime juice and cumin. Season with salt and pepper to taste. Stir to combine.

Toast 4 slices of rye bread until golden. Spoon 1/4 of the avocado mixture onto each slice of bread. Top with a poached egg and serve immediately.

Avocado and Olive Paste on Toasted Rye Bread

Serves: 4

Prep time: 5 min

Ingredients:

1 avocado, halved, peeled and finely chopped

1 tbsp green onions, finely chopped

2 tbsp green olive paste

1 tbsp lemon juice

Directions:

Mash avocados with a fork or potato masher until almost smooth. Add the onions, green olive paste and lemon juice. Season with salt and pepper to taste. Stir to combine.

Toast 4 slices of rye bread until golden. Spoon 1/4 of the avocado mixture onto each slice of bread.

Avocado, Lettuce and Tomato Sandwiches

Serves: 2

Prep time: 3-4 min

Ingredients:

4 slices rye bread

1 tbsp mayonnaise

1 tbsp basil pesto

2 large leaves lettuce

1/2 tomato, thinly sliced

1/2 avocado, peeled and sliced

6 very thin slices cucumber

Directions:

Combine mayonnaise and pesto. Spread this mixture on the four slices of bread.

Layer two slices with one lettuce leaf, two slices tomato, two slices avocado and three slices cucumber. Top with remaining bread slices. Cut sandwiches in half diagonally and serve.

Avocado and Chickpea Sandwiches

Serves: 4

Prep time: 3-4 min

Ingredients:

4 slices white bread

1/2 cup canned chickpeas

1 small avocado

2 green onions, finely chopped

1 egg, hard boiled

1/2 tomato, thinly sliced

1/2 cucumber, thinly sliced

salt, to taste

Directions:

Mash the avocado and chickpeas with a fork or potato masher until smooth. Add in green onions and salt and combine well.

Spread this mixture on the four slices of bread. Top each slice with tomato, cucumber and egg, and serve.

Avocado, Roast Beef and Lettuce Sandwiches

Serves: 2

Prep time: 3-4 min

Ingredients:

4 slices rye bread

1 tbsp mayonnaise

4 oz quality roast beef, thinly sliced

1/2 avocado, peeled and sliced

2 large leaves lettuce

1/2 tomato, thinly sliced

Directions:

Spread mayonnaise on the four slices of bread.

Layer two slices with roast beef, one lettuce leaf, two slices tomato and two slices avocado. Top with remaining bread slices and serve.

Avocado Gazpacho

Serves 4

Prep time: 5 min

Ingredients:

2 ripe avocados, peeled and chopped

2-3 tomatoes, diced

1 large cucumber, peeled and diced

1/2 small onion, chopped

2 tbsp lemon juice

1 tsp salt

black pepper, to taste

fresh parsley leaves, finely cut, to serve

Directions:

Combine avocados, cucumbers, tomatoes, onion, lemon juice, salt and black pepper in a blender. P

process until smooth and serve sprinkled with chopped parsley leaves.

Avocado and Cucumber Soup

Serves 4

Prep time: 5 min

Ingredients:

2 ripe avocados, peeled and chopped

3 cucumbers, peeled and chopped

1 green onion, chopped

2 tbsp lime juice

1/2 tsp salt

black pepper, to taste

fresh coriander leaves, finely cut, to serve

Directions:

Combine avocados, cucumbers, onion, lime juice, salt and black pepper in a blender.

Process until smooth and serve sprinkled with chopped coriander leaves.

Warm Chicken and Avocado Soup

Serves 4

Prep time: 6-7 min

Ingredients:

2 ripe avocados, peeled and chopped

1 cooked chicken breast, shredded

1 garlic clove, chopped

3 cups chicken broth

salt and black pepper, to taste

fresh coriander leaves, finely cut, to serve

1/2 cup sour cream, to serve

Directions:

Combine avocados, garlic, and chicken broth in a blender. Process until smooth and transfer to a saucepan. Add in chicken and cook, stirring, over medium heat until the mixture is hot.

Serve topped with sour cream and finely cut coriander leaves.

Avocado and Arugula Pasta

Serves: 4

Prep time: 5 min

Ingredients:

3 cups cooked bow tie pasta

½ cup cooked corn kernels

1 large avocado, peeled and diced

1 cup baby arugula leaves

2 tbsp basil pesto

3 tbsp olive oil

3 tbsp lemon juice

½ cup grated Parmesan cheese

Directions:

Whisk olive oil, lemon juice, basil pesto and half the Parmesan cheese in a small bowl. Season with salt and pepper to taste.

Combine pasta, avocado, corn and baby arugula. Add oil mixture and toss to combine. Serve with remaining Parmesan cheese.

Creamy Avocado and Chicken Spaghetti

Serves: 5-6

Prep time: 20 min

Ingredients:

12 oz spaghetti

1 cup cooked chicken, shredded

2 avocados, peeled and diced

1 cup cherry tomatoes, halved

1 garlic clove, chopped

2 tbsp basil pesto

5 tbsp olive oil

4 tbsp lemon juice

1/4 cup grated Parmesan cheese

Directions:

In a large pot of boiling salted water, cook spaghetti according to package instructions. Drain and set aside in a large bowl.

In a blender, combine lemon juice, garlic, basil pesto and avocados and blend until smooth.

Combine spaghetti, chicken, cherry tomatoes and avocado sauce. Sprinkle with Parmesan cheese and serve immediately.

Avocado, Roasted Mushroom and Ham Spaghetti

Serves: 5-6

Prep time: 20 min

Ingredients:

12 oz spaghetti

1 cup ham, cut in cubes

2 avocados, peeled and diced

10-15 white mushrooms, halved

2 tbsp green olive paste

2 garlic cloves, chopped

olive oil spay

salt and black pepper, to taste

1/4 cup grated Parmesan cheese

Directions:

Line a baking tray with baking paper and place mushrooms on it. Spray with olive oil and season with salt and black pepper to taste. Roast in a preheated to 375 F oven for 15 minutes, or until golden and tender.

In a large pot of boiling salted water, cook spaghetti according to package instructions. Drain and set aside in a large bowl.

In a blender, combine lemon juice, garlic, olive paste and avocados and blend until smooth.

Combine pasta, diced ham, mushrooms and avocado sauce. Sprinkle with Parmesan cheese and serve immediately.

Avocado and Chicken Risotto

Serves: 4

Prep time: 15 min

Ingredients:

3 cups chicken broth

2 chicken breasts, diced

1 cup risotto Rice

2 avocados, peeled and diced

3 tbsp extra virgin olive oil

1 onion, finely chopped

2 garlic cloves, crushed

2 tbsp raisins

1 cup grated Parmesan cheese, plus extra to serve

5-6 green onions, finely cut, to serve

Directions:

Place chicken broth in a saucepan, bring to the boil, then reduce heat to low and keep at a simmer.

In a non-stick frypan, cook chicken for 5-6 minutes each side, or until browned and cooked through. Transfer to a plate

In the same pan, heat olive oil over medium heat. Add the onion and cook, stirring, for 1-2 minutes until softened. Stir in the garlic, then add the rice and cook, stirring, for 1 minute to coat the grains.

Add the broth, a spoonful at a time, stirring occasionally, allowing each spoonful to be absorbed before adding the next. Simmer until all liquid has absorbed and rice is tender. Stir in the chicken,

Parmesan cheese and raisins, then cover and remove from the heat.

Serve in bowls topped with diced avocados, extra Parmesan cheese and chopped green onions.

Cornmeal Avocado Muffin Recipe

Serves: 12

Prep time: 20 min

Ingredients:

1 cup whole wheat flour

1 cup cornmeal

1/4 cup sugar

3 eggs

1 tsp baking powder

1 tsp baking soda

1 tsp salt

1 cup milk

1/3 cup mashed avocado

1/2 cup Cheddar cheese

Directions:

Preheat oven to 375 F. Grease 12 muffin tin wells or line with paper cups.

In a large bowl, whisk together the cornmeal, whole wheat flour, sugar, baking powder, baking soda and salt.

In a separate bowl, whisk together the eggs, milk and mashed avocado. Combine with avocado mixture; do not over-mix. Stir in 1/2 cup Cheddar cheese.

Spoon batter into prepared muffin tin; bake 15-18 minutes or until tops start to brown and a toothpick inserted into a muffin comes out clean.

Avocado and Banana Muffins

Serves: 12

Prep time: 20 min

Ingredients:

1/2 cup mashed avocado

1/2 cup mashed bananas

2 large eggs

1/2 cup milk

2 cups all-purpose flour

1 cup sugar

1 tsp baking soda

1 tsp salt

1/2 cup chocolate chips

Directions:

Preheat oven to 375 F. Grease 12 muffin tin wells or line with paper cups.

In a large bowl, mix avocado, bananas, eggs and milk. In a separate bowl, whisk flour, sugar, baking soda and salt. Combine with avocado mixture; do not over-mix. Stir in chocolate chips.

Spoon batter into prepared muffin tin; bake 15-18 minutes or until tops start to brown and a toothpick inserted into a muffin comes out clean.

Avocado and Pumpkin Muffins

Serves: 13-14

Prep time: 20 min

Ingredients:

1/2 cup mashed avocado

11/2 cup pumpkin puree

2 large eggs

2 cups all-purpose flour

1 cup sugar

1 tsp baking soda

1 tsp salt

1 tsp cinnamon

1 tsp vanilla

1/2 cup walnuts, chopped

Directions:

Preheat oven to 375 F. Grease 12 muffin tin wells or line with paper cups.

In a large bowl, mix avocado, pumpkin and eggs. In a separate bowl, whisk flour, sugar, baking soda, cinnamon, vanilla and salt. Combine with avocado mixture; do not over-mix. Stir in walnuts.

Spoon batter into prepared muffin tin; bake 15-18 minutes or until tops start to brown and a toothpick inserted into a muffin comes out clean.

Green Apple and Avocado Smoothie

Serves: 2-3

Prep time: 5 min

Ingredients:

3-4 ice cubes

1 avocado, peeled and chopped

1 cup orange juice

3 green apples, peeled and chopped

1 cup parsley leaves

juice from 1 lime

Directions:

Place all ingredients in a blender and purée until smooth.

Carrot, Mango and Avocado Smoothie

Serves: 2-3

Prep time: 5 min

Ingredients:

1 1/2 cup frozen mango chunks

1 avocado, peeled and chopped

1 cup carrot juice

½ cup orange juice

1 tsp grated ginger

Directions:

Combine all ingredients in a blender and blend until smooth.

Strawberry, Coconut and Avocado Smoothie

Serves: 2-3

Prep time: 5 min

Ingredients:

3-4 ice cubes

1 avocado, peeled and diced

2 cups coconut milk

3 cups fresh strawberries

Directions:

Place all ingredients in a blender and purée until smooth.

Delicious Avocado and Plum Smoothie

Serves: 2-3

Prep time: 5 min

Ingredients:

3-4 ice cubes

1/2 avocado, peeled and chopped

1 cup coconut milk

6 plums, pitted and chopped

½ tsp cinnamon

Directions:

Combine ingredients in blender and blend until smooth.

Pumpkin and Avocado Smoothie

Serves: 2-3

Prep time: 5 min

Ingredients:

3-4 ice cubes

1 avocado, peeled and chopped

1 cups orange juice

1 pear, chopped

½ cup cooked pumpkin

½ tsp cinnamon

1 tsp grated ginger

Directions:

Combine ingredients in blender and purée until smooth.

Pineapple and Avocado Smoothie

Serves: 2-3

Prep time: 5 min

Ingredients:

2-3 ice cubes

1 avocado, peeled and chopped

1 cup apple juice

1 cup seedless grapes

1 cup diced pineapple

Directions:

Combine ingredients in a blender and purée until smooth.

Kiwi, Grapes and Avocado Smoothie

Serves: 2-3

Prep time: 5 min

Ingredients:

2-3 ice cubes

1 cup orange juice

½ avocado, peeled and chopped

2 kiwi, peeled and chopped

1 cup seedless green grapes

Directions:

Combine all ingredients in a blender and purée until smooth.

Avocado and Nectarine Smoothie

Serves: 2-3

Prep time: 5 min

Ingredients:

1/2 cup crushed ice

1 avocado, peeled and diced

2 cups orange juice

2 ripe nectarines, chopped

2-3 dates

Directions:

Combine all ingredients in a blender and purée until smooth.

FREE BONUS RECIPES: 20 Superfood Paleo and Vegan Smoothies for Vibrant Health and Easy Weight Loss

Kale and Kiwi Smoothie

Serves: 2

Prep time: 2-3 min

Ingredients:

2-3 ice cubes

1 cup orange juice

1 small pear, peeled and chopped

2 kiwi, peeled and chopped

2-3 kale leaves

2-3 dates, pitted

Directions:

Combine all ingredients in a high speed blender and blend until smooth.

Delicious Broccoli Smoothie

Serves: 2

Prep time: 2-3 min

Ingredients:

2-3 frozen broccoli florets

1 cup coconut milk

1 banana, peeled and chopped

1 cup pineapple, cut

1 peach, chopped

1 tsp cinnamon

Directions:

Combine all ingredients in a high speed blender and blend until smooth.

Papaya Smoothie

Serves: 2

Prep time: 2-3 min

Ingredients:

2-3 frozen broccoli florets

1 cup orange juice

1 small ripe avocado, peeled, cored and diced

1 cup papaya

1 cup fresh strawberries

Directions:

Combine all ingredients in a high speed blender and blend until smooth.

Beet and Papaya Smoothie

Serves: 2

Prep time: 2-3 min

Ingredients:

3-4 ice cubes

1 cup orange juice

1 banana, peeled and chopped

1 cup papaya

1 small beet, peeled and cut

Directions:

Combine all ingredients in a high speed blender and blend until smooth.

Lean Green Smoothie

Serves: 2

Prep time: 2-3 min

Ingredients:

1 frozen banana, chopped

1 cup orange juice

2-3 kale leaves, stems removed

1 small cucumber, peeled and chopped

1/2 cup fresh parsley leaves

½ tsp grated ginger

Directions:

Combine all ingredients in a high speed blender and blend until smooth.

Easy Antioxidant Smoothie

Serves: 2

Prep time: 2-3 min

Ingredients:

2-3 frozen broccoli florets

1 cup orange juice

2 plums, cut

1 cup raspberries

1 tsp ginger powder

Directions:

Combine all ingredients in a high speed blender and blend until smooth.

Healthy Purple Smoothie

Serves: 2

Prep time: 2-3 min

Ingredients:

2-3 frozen broccoli florets

1 cup water

1/2 avocado, peeled and chopped

3 plums, chopped

1 cup blueberries

Directions:

Combine all ingredients in a high speed blender and blend until smooth.

Mom's Favorite Kale Smoothie

Serves: 2

Prep time: 2-3 min

Ingredients:

2-3 ice cubes

1½ cup orange juice

1 green small apple, cut

½ cucumber, chopped

2-3 leaves kale

½ cup raspberries

Directions:

Combine all ingredients in a high speed blender and blend until smooth.

Creamy Green Smoothie

Serves: 2

Prep time: 2-3 min

Ingredients:

1 frozen banana

1 cup coconut milk

1 small pear, chopped

1 cup baby spinach

1 cup grapes

1 tbsp coconut butter

1 tsp vanilla extract

Directions:

Combine all ingredients in a high speed blender and blend until smooth.

Strawberry and Arugula Smoothie

Serves: 2

Prep time: 2-3 min

Ingredients:

2 cups frozen strawberries

1 cup unsweetened almond milk

10-12 arugula leaves

1/2 tsp ground cinnamon

Directions:

Combine ice, almond milk, strawberries, arugula and cinnamon in a high speed blender. Blend until smooth and serve.

Emma's Amazing Smoothie

Serves: 2

Prep time: 2-3 min

Ingredients:

1 frozen banana, chopped

1 cup orange juice

1 large nectarine, sliced

1/2 zucchini, peeled and chopped

2-3 dates, pitted

Directions:

Combine all ingredients in a high speed blender and blend until smooth.

Good-To-Go Morning Smoothie

Serves: 2

Prep time: 2-3 min

Ingredients:

1 cup frozen strawberries

1 cup apple juice

1 banana, chopped

1 cup raw asparagus, chopped

1 tbsp ground flaxseed

Directions:

Combine all ingredients in a high speed blender and blend until smooth.

Endless Energy Smoothie

Serves: 2

Prep time: 2-3 min

Ingredients:

1 frozen banana, chopped

11/2 cup green tea

1 cup chopped pineapple

2 raw asparagus spears, chopped

1 lime, juiced

1 tbsp chia seeds

Directions:

Combine all ingredients in a high speed blender and blend until smooth.

High-fibre Fruit Smoothie

Serves: 2

Prep time: 2-3 min

Ingredients:

1 frozen banana, chopped

1 cup orange juice

2 cups chopped papaya

1 cup shredded cabbage

1 tbsp chia seeds

Directions:

Combine all ingredients in a high speed blender and blend until smooth.

Nutritious Green Smoothie

Serves: 2

Prep time: 2-3 min

Ingredients:

2-3 frozen broccoli florets

1 cup apple juice

1 large pear, chopped

1 kiwi, peeled and chopped

1 cup spinach leaves

1-2 dates, pitted

Directions:

Combine all ingredients in a high speed blender and blend until smooth.

Apricot, Strawberry and Banana Smoothie

Serves: 2

Prep time: 2-3 min

Ingredients:

1 frozen banana

11/2 cup almond milk

5 dried apricots

1 cup fresh strawberries

Directions:

Combine all ingredients in a high speed blender and blend until smooth.

Spinach and Green Apple Smoothie

Serves: 2

Prep time: 2-3 min

Ingredients:

3-4 ice cubes

1 cup unsweetened almond milk

1 banana, peeled and chopped

2 green apples, peeled and chopped

1 cup raw spinach leaves

3-4 dates, pitted

1 tsp grated ginger

Directions:

Combine all ingredients in a high speed blender and blend until smooth.

Superfood Blueberry Smoothie

Serves: 2

Prep time: 2-3 min

Ingredients:

2-3 cubes frozen spinach

1 cup green tea

1 banana

2 cups blueberries

1 tbsp ground flaxseed

Directions:

Combine all ingredients in a high speed blender and blend until smooth.

Zucchini and Blueberry Smoothie

Serves: 2

Prep time: 2-3 min

Ingredients:

1 cup frozen blueberries

1 cup unsweetened almond milk

1 banana

1 zucchini, peeled and chopped

Directions:

Combine all ingredients in a high speed blender and blend until smooth.

Tropical Spinach Smoothie

Serves: 2

Prep time: 2-3 min

Ingredients:

1/2 cup crushed ice or 3-4 ice cubes

1 cup coconut milk

1 mango, peeled and diced

1 cup fresh spinach leaves

4-5 dates, pitted

1/2 tsp vanilla extract

Directions:

Combine all ingredients in a high speed blender and blend until smooth.

About the Author

Alissa Grey is a fitness and nutrition enthusiast who loves to teach people about losing weight and feeling better about themselves. She lives in a small French village in the foothills of a beautiful mountain range with her husband, three teenage kids, two free spirited dogs, and various other animals.

Alissa Grey is incredibly lucky to be able to cook and eat natural foods, mostly grown nearby, something she's done since she was a teenager. She enjoys yoga, running, reading, hanging out with her family, and growing organic vegetables and herbs.

Made in the USA
Monee, IL
09 March 2022

92562974R00049